Change for Chessie

Tracey's Elementary School

Media Coin Drive

Spring 2007

DRAGONFLIES

INSECTS DISCOVERY LIBRARY

Jason Cooper

Rourke Publishing LLC
Vero Beach, Florida 32964

www.rourkepublishing.com

PHOTO CREDITS: All photos © Lynn M. Stone except p. 19 © James P. Rowan

Title page: Dewdrops cover a dragonfly's wings.

Library of Congress Cataloging-in-Publication Data

Cooper, Jason, 1942-
  Dragonflies / Jason Cooper.
      p. cm. -- (Insects discovery library)
  Includes bibliographical references.
  ISBN 1-59515-426-4 (hardcover)
  1. Dragonflies--Juvenile literature. I. Title.
  QL520.C66 2006
  595.7'33--dc22
                              2005010969

Printed in the USA

CG/CG

Rourke Publishing

www.rourkepublishing.com – sales@rourkepublishing.com
Post Office Box 3328, Vero Beach, FL 32964

1-800-394-7055

TABLE OF CONTENTS

Dragonflies

Dragonflies are big, colorful **insects**. They are not named for their beauty. They are named for the fierce, flying dragons of **legend**.

Dragonflies are like rainbows with wings.

Dragonflies are **predators**. Predators eat other animals. Dragonflies eat other insects.

Dragonflies are close cousins of damselflies. There are 6,000 kinds of dragonflies and damselflies.

A dragonfly waits on a perch.

This damselfly is wet with morning dew.

Did You Know?

Dragonflies are called skimmers, darters, chasers, and "darning needles."

Looking at Dragonflies

Dragonflies' shiny bodies may be bright green or red. They may be blue or another color. Dragonfly wings are all or partly clear.

A green clearwing dragonfly lands on a swamp lily.

A dragonfly body has three main parts. It has a head with two large eyes. It has a **thorax**. It has a long, slender **abdomen**.

The thorax is the middle part. A dragonfly's six legs and four wings grow from the thorax.

A dragonfly's three major body parts from top to bottom: head, thorax, and abdomen.

Dragonfly Food

Dragonflies **zigzag** speedily through the air to catch flying insects. A few kinds of dragonflies catch their **prey** on the ground.

Toads, frogs, fish, and birds dine on dragonflies.

Bullfrogs are predators of dragonflies.

12

Where Dragonflies Live

Dragonflies live all over the world except in very, cold places. Most kinds of dragonflies live in very warm countries.

This damselfly lives in the warmth of Central America.

Dragonflies live near water. They like lakes and marshes. They also like waterfall pools and ponds.

This dragonfly lives in a marsh.

Young Dragonflies

Dragonflies and damselflies lay their eggs on or in water. Baby dragonflies called **nymphs** hatch from the eggs. Nymphs live and hunt in the water.

This dragonfly nymph's wings have just begun to grow.

A damselfly lays her eggs.

Some kinds of dragonflies are nymphs for just days. Others are nymphs for up to six years! Nymphs grow into adult dragonflies.

Dragonfly nymphs become adult dragonflies.

GLOSSARY

abdomen (AB duh mun) — the third main part of an insect after the head and thorax

insects (IN SEKTZ) — small, boneless animals with six legs

legend (LEJ und) — a story that has come down from the past

nymphs (NIMFZ) — a young stage of life in certain insects, before they become adults

predators (PRED uh turz) — animals that hunt other animals for food

prey (PRAY) — any animal caught and eaten by another animal

thorax (THOR aks) — the second main body part of an insect after the head and before the abdomen

zigzag (ZIG ZAG) — to fly through the air in short, jumpy movements

Damselflies are harmless to people.

INDEX

Further Reading

Morris, Tim. *Dragonfly*. Smart Apple Media, 2004

Pringle, Laurence. *Dragon in the Sky: The Story of a Green Darner*. Scholastic, 2001

Websites to Visit

http://powell.colgate.edu/wda/Beginners_Guide.htm

http://dragonflywebsite.com

About the Author

Jason Cooper has written many children's books for Rourke Publishing about a variety of topics. Cooper travels widely to gather information for his books.